# African Wildlife from A to Z

### Animal Kingdom ABCs

## A Photo Journey
## Exploring the Fascinating
## Creatures of Africa with Fun Facts
## for Kids Who Love Wild Animals

### by Michele Renee Acosta

Published by
Just Because...Books
an imprint of
My Extra Umbrella

*African Wildlife from A to Z:*
*A Photo Journey Exploring the Fascinating Creatures of Africa*
*with Fun Facts for Kids Who Love Wild Animals*
Copyright © 2025 by Michele Renee Acosta

Library of Congress Cataloging-in-Publication Data is available.
Library of Congress Control Number: 2024922753

ISBN (hardcover): 979-8-89615-061-9
ISBN (paperback): 979-8-89615-001-5
ISBN (ebook–Kindle edition): 979-8-89615-008-4
ISBN (ebook–EPUB edition): 979-8-89615-068-8

Published by
Just Because...Books
an imprint of My Extra Umbrella
1968 South Coast Highway
Suite 891
Laguna Beach, California 92651
Publisher@MyExtraUmbrella.com

This is Book 1 in the *Animal Kingdom ABCs* series.

Books in the *Animal Kingdom ABCs* series can be read in any order.

Printed in Laguna Beach, California, U.S.A.

First Edition

# Author's Note

Welcome to *African Wildlife from A to Z*, a book that invites young children to embark on an exciting adventure through Africa's diverse wildlife. This book, part of the *Animal Kingdom ABCs* series, is designed to introduce children to wildlife from across the African continent in a way that's both fun and engaging. While it may look like a traditional ABC book, it goes far beyond teaching the alphabet. Instead, it's a window into the fascinating world of the animals and other wildlife that inhabit this unique part of the globe.

Each book in the series is organized alphabetically, which helps young pre-readers easily follow along and engage with the content. However, it's not about "learning the ABCs" in the usual sense. Rather, it's about sparking curiosity about wildlife and showing how vast and varied the animal kingdom can be, one letter at a time. Many of the wildlife names in this book—like *quelea* and *xenopus*—are not words typically found in a traditional ABC book. That's part of the fun! While these words may be challenging to pronounce, it's a great way for children to expand their vocabulary and learn about creatures they might never have encountered before.

Before reading for the first time, I encourage you to have a conversation about the animals children might expect to see in a book about African wildlife. Ask children to share what they already know about animals in general and African animals in particular. At the end of the book, you'll find fun facts about African wildlife, as well as critical-thinking questions designed to inspire deeper conversations. These questions are perfect for further exploration of the topic and for encouraging curiosity and a life-long love of learning.

Remember, the goal of this book is discovery and wonder. It's okay if the animal names are tricky—that's why I included helpful pronunciations and facts! This book, and the series as a whole, aims to offer children an opportunity to explore the natural world continent by continent, fostering a sense of adventure, awe, and connection to the animals with which we share this planet.

Thank you for joining me on this exciting adventure through Africa's animal kingdom!

*Happy exploring!*

Michele Renee Acosta

If you love *African Wildlife from A to Z*, explore the rest of the *Animal Kingdom ABCs* series. Each book features real animals, surprising facts, and fun ways to spark curiosity. You'll also find other fiction and nonfiction series for children ages 3–8, along with a little something extra to download and enjoy.

**A**

**African Buffalo**

**B**

# Bonobo

# C

# Cheetah

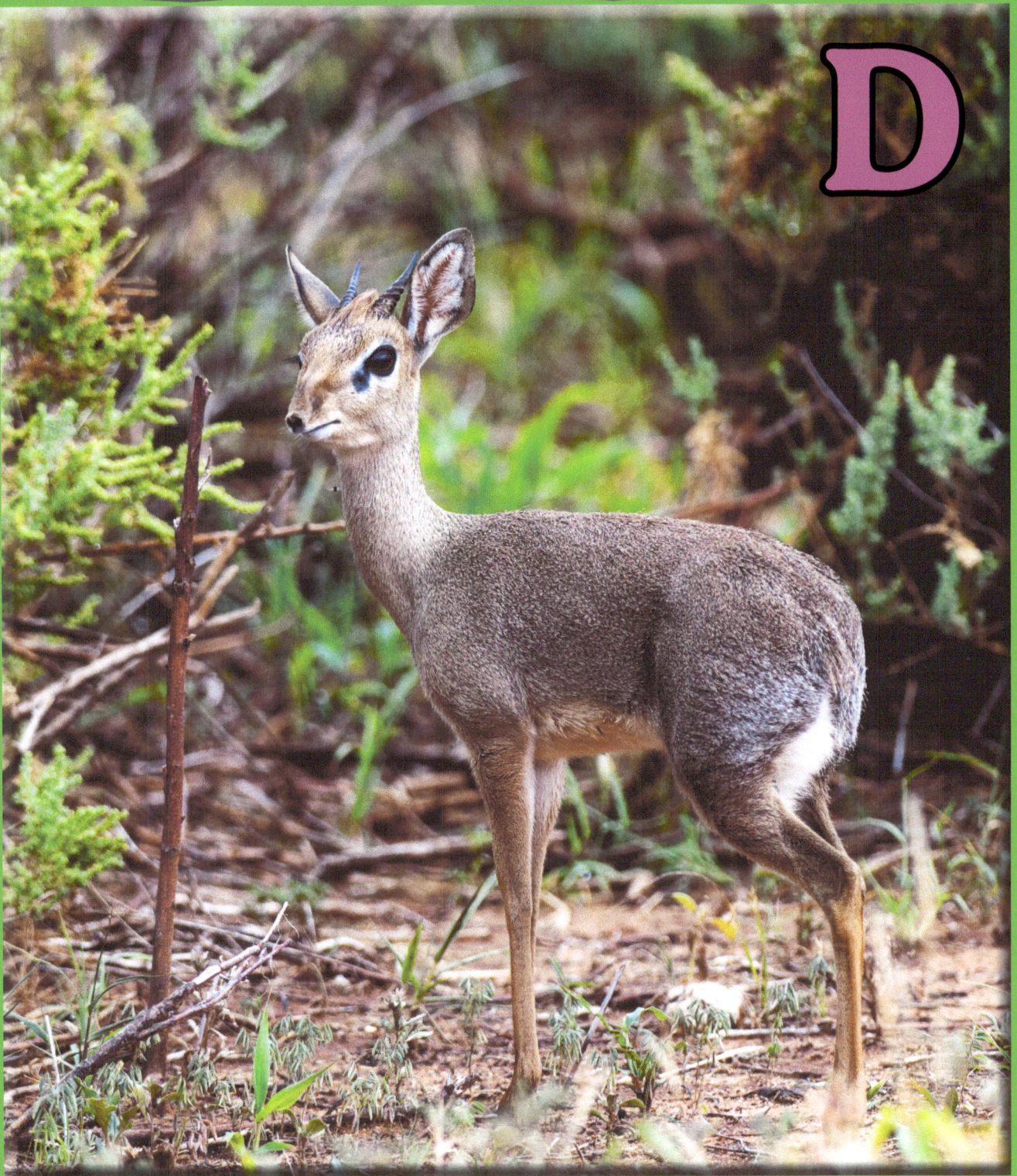

**D**

# Dik-Dik

# E

# Elephant

**F**

**F**lamingo

**G**

# Gorilla

**H**

# Hippopotamus

**I**

# Impala

# J

**J**ackal

# K

# Kudu

**L**

# Lion

# M

**Meerkat**

**N**

# Nile Crocodile

# O

# Ostrich

**P**

# **P**atas Monkey

# Q

Quelea

# Rhinoceros

# S

## Serval

**T**

# **T**opi

# U

## Uganda Kob

**V**

# **V**ervet Monkey

# W

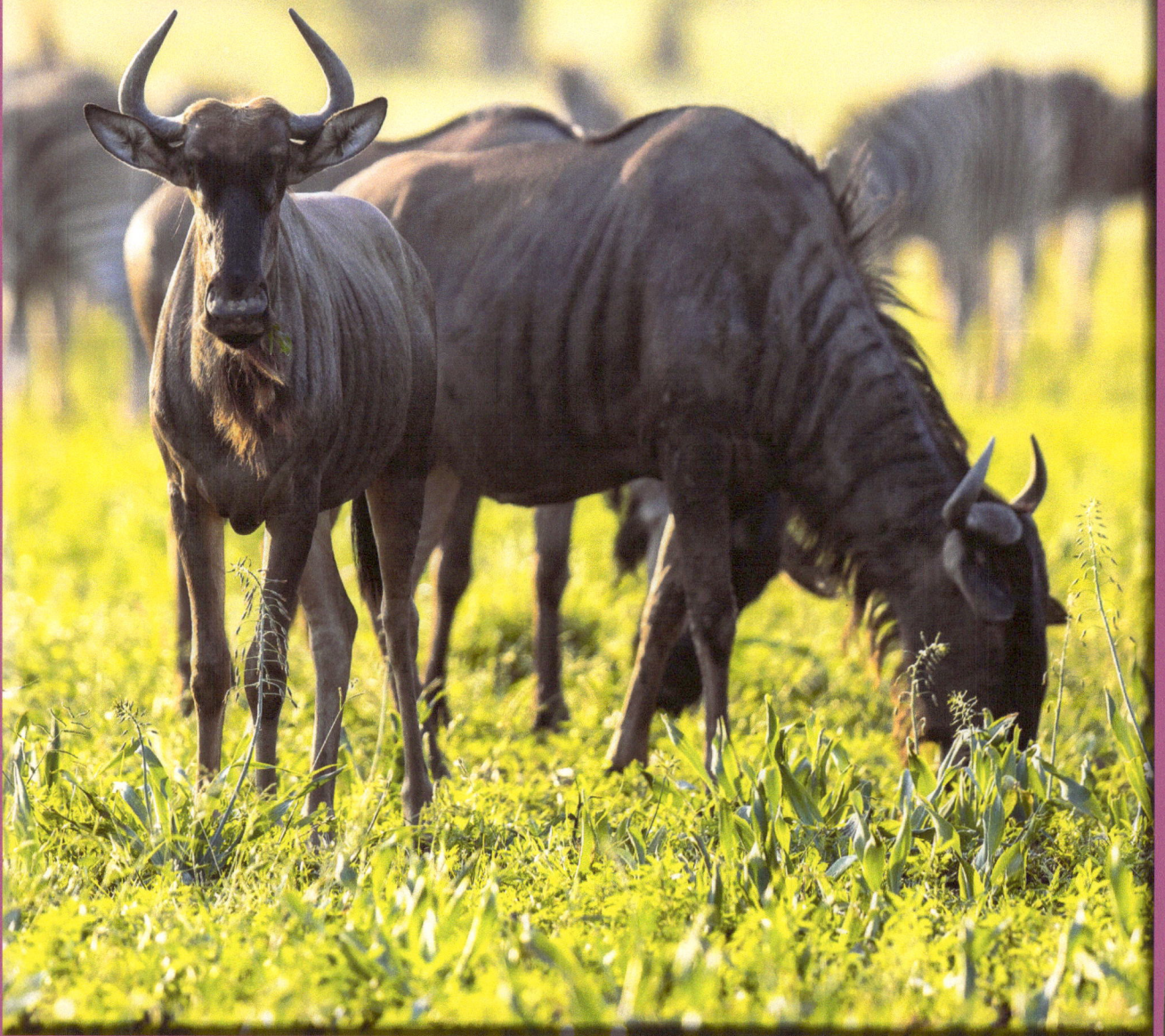

# Wildebeest

# **X**enopus

# Y

## Yellow Baboon

# Z

# Zebra

# Would You Believe?

**African Buffalo** work together to stay safe by circling around weaker members of the herd.

**Bonobos** share about 98.7 percent of their DNA with humans, making them our closest living relatives.

**Cheetahs** don't roar! They chirp, squeak, and even purr.

**Dik-Diks** mark their territory using tiny scent glands near their eyes.

**Elephants** are among the smartest animals on Earth. They can recognize themselves in mirrors!

**Flamingos** turn pink because of the food they eat. They love shrimp and algae!

**Gorillas** build a fresh nest to sleep in every night. They build their nests on the ground or in trees.

**Hippopotamuses** have a natural pink "sunscreen" that helps protect their skin.

**Impala** can leap as far as a school bus in a single jump!

**Jackals** sometimes follow birds like hornbills to help find food.

**Kudu** have large, swiveling ears that help them hear even the faintest sounds from faraway.

**Lions** rest or nap most of the day—sometimes up to 20 hours!

**Meerkats** take turns standing guard while the others search for food.

**Nile Crocodiles** store fat in their tails, allowing them to go for several months without eating.

**Ostriches** have the biggest eyes of any animal that lives on land.

**Patas Monkeys** can run faster than any other monkey and as fast as a car driving 34 miles per hour!

**Queleas** fly together in flocks so big they can look like clouds.

**Rhinoceroses** skin can be almost two inches thick, but they still need to keep cool in the heat.

**Servals** can jump up to nine feet straight up to catch prey high in the air.

**Topi** climb onto little hills or mounds to watch for danger.

**Uganda Kobs** sometimes face each other to show who is stronger.

**Vervet Monkeys** have special calls to warn about different animals nearby.

**Wildebeests** travel 500 to 1,000 miles each year during their seasonal migrations.

**Xenopus** (also called African Clawed Frogs) can grow back lost body parts.

**Yellow Baboons** show friendship by helping each other stay clean.

**Zebras** have stripes as unique as human fingerprints. No two look exactly the same!

# What Do You Know?

Use these questions to spark curiosity and conversation. Talk about details you notice in the photos and what you've learned together from *Would You Believe?* facts and other sources.

1. Which African animal surprised you most?
   What about that animal is most interesting to you?

2. Which animal do you think would be easiest to spot in the wild?
   Which animal do you think would be hardest to spot? Why?

3. Which African animal would you want to see up close? Why?

4. How do animals like monkeys, meerkats, and African buffalo help each other stay safe?

5. How might big ears help an animal in the wild?

6. Which African animals do you think are fast runners? Which animals do you think are great jumpers? Why?

7. What do you think animals that live on wide open grasslands might have in common?

8. Which African animals do you think live in groups? Which ones might live alone?
   What clues helped you decide?

9. Pick an African animal. How do you think this animal protects itself from danger?

10. If you made up a new African animal, where would it live and what would it eat?

11. Which animals do you think make loud sounds? Which animals might make quiet sounds?

12. If you could be one African animal for a day, which animal would you choose? Why?

# How Do You Say It?

**African Buffalo** (AF-ri-kuhn BUH-fuh-loh)
**Bonobo** (boh-NOH-boh)
**Cheetah** (CHEE-tuh)
**Dik-Dik** (DIHK-DIHK)
**Elephant** (EL-uh-fuhnt)
**Flamingo** (fluh-MING-goh)
**Gorilla** (guh-RIL-uh)
**Hippopotamus** (HIP-uh-POT-uh-muhs)
**Impala** (im-PAH-luh)
**Jackal** (JAK-uhl)
**Kudu** (KOO-doo)
**Lion** (LY-uhn)
**Meerkat** (MEER-kat)

**Nile Crocodile** (NYL KROK-uh-dyl)
**Ostrich** (OS-trij)
**Patas Monkey** (PAH-tahs MUNG-kee)
**Quelea** (KWEE-lee-uh)
**Rhinoceros** (rye-NOS-er-uhs)
**Serval** (SUR-vuhl)
**Topi** (TOH-pee)
**Uganda Kob** (yoo-GAN-duh KOB)
**Vervet Monkey** (VUR-vit MUNG-kee)
**Wildebeest** (WIL-duh-beest)
**Xenopus** (ZEE-nuh-puhs)
**Yellow Baboon** (YEL-oh buh-BOON)
**Zebra** (ZEE-bruh)

**Sources** African Wildlife Foundation (https://www.awf.org); BBC Earth (https://www.bbcearth.com); National Geographic (https://www.nationalgeographic.com/animals); National Geographic Kids: National Geographic Partners (https://kids.nationalgeographic.com/animals); San Diego Zoo Kids: San Diego Zoo Wildlife Alliance (https://kids.sandiegozoo.org); Sabi Sabi Reserve: Wildlife & Nature (https://www.sabisabi.com); Smithsonian's National Zoo & Conservation Biology Institute: Animal Index (https://nationalzoo.si.edu/animals); World Wildlife Fund (https://www.worldwildlife.org/species); African Wildlife Foundation: Great Migration (https://www.awf.org)

More animals.
More fun.
More to explore.

www.ingramcontent.com/pod-product-compliance
Lightning Source LLC
Chambersburg PA
CBHW061204030426

42338CB00015B/1534